TOOLS FOR TEACHERS

- **ATOS:** 0.6
- **GRL:** C
- **WORD COUNT:** 26
- **CURRICULUM CONNECTIONS:** animals, habitats

Skills to Teach

- **HIGH-FREQUENCY WORDS:** are, by, mom, stay, the, these, they, what
- **CONTENT WORDS:** babies, den, forest, fox, kits, learn, play, run, sleep
- **PUNCTUATION:** exclamation point, periods, question mark
- **WORD STUDY:** long /a/, spelled *ay* (*play*, *stay*); long /e/, spelled ee (*sleep*); r-controlled vowels (*learn*)
- **TEXT TYPE:** information report

Before Reading Activities

- Read the title and give a simple statement of the main idea.
- Have students "walk" though the book and talk about what they see in the pictures.
- Introduce new vocabulary by having students predict the first letter and locate the word in the text.
- Discuss any unfamiliar concepts that are in the text.

After Reading Activities

The book's text tells us that fox kits are playful. They play with their siblings. They learn from their mother. Ask the children how fox kits are similar to human children. What actions do they do that are similar? How are they different? What other actions do fox kits do that are not mentioned in the text? Make a list with the headings "similarities" and "differences." Write their answers under each heading. Discuss their answers as a group.

Tadpole Books are published by Jump!, 5357 Penn Avenue South, Minneapolis, MN 55419, www.jumplibrary.com

Editor: Jenna Trnka **Designer:** Anna Peterson

Photo Credits: Stockbyte/Getty, cover; UroshPetrovic/iStock, 1; Milan Zygmunt/Shutterstock, 2–3, 16tm; Richard Seeley/Shutterstock, 4–5; Geoffrey Kuchera/Shutterstock, 6–7, 16tl; cynoclub/Shutterstock, 8–9, 16br; Mikael Males/Dreamstime, 10–11, 16bl; Chase Dekker/Shutterstock, 12–13, 16bm; James Hager/Getty, 14–15, 16tr.

Library of Congress Cataloging-in-Publication Data
Names: Nilsen, Genevieve, author.
Title: Fox kits / by Genevieve Nilsen.
Description: (Tadpole edition). | Minneapolis, MN : Jump!, Inc., (2018) | Series: Forest babies | Includes index.
Identifiers: LCCN 2017061702 (print) | LCCN 2018007262 (ebook) | ISBN 9781624969638 (ebook) | ISBN 9781624969614 (hardcover : alk. paper) | ISBN 9781624969621 (pbk.)
Subjects: LCSH: Foxes—Infancy—Juvenile literature.
Classification: LCC QL737.C22 (ebook) | LCC QL737.C22 N55 2018 (print) | DDC 599.77513/92—dc23
LC record available at https://lccn.loc.gov/2017061702

FOREST BABIES

FOX KITS

by Genevieve Nilsen

TABLE OF CONTENTS

tadpole books

FOX KITS

What are these forest babies?

Fox kits!

mom

They stay by mom.

They stay by the den.

They sleep.

They play.

They run.

They learn.

WORDS TO KNOW

den

kits

learn

play

run

sleep

INDEX